Brilliant Birds

Thea Feldman

KINGFISHER

First published 2015 by Kingfisher
an imprint of Macmillan Children's Books
a division of Macmillan Children's Publishers Limited
20 New Wharf Road, London N1 9RR
Basingstoke and Oxford
Associated companies throughout the world
www.panmacmillan.com

Series editor: Polly Goodman
Literacy consultant: Hilary Horton

ISBN: 978-0-7534-3666-0
Copyright © Macmillan Publishers Ltd 2015

9 8 7 6 5 4 3 2 1
1TR/1014/WKT/UG/105MA

A CIP catalogue record for this book is available from the British Library.

Printed in China

Picture credits
The Publisher would like to thank the following for permission to reproduce their
material. Every care has been taken to trace copyright holders. However, if there
have been unintentional omissions or failure to trace copyright holders, we apologize
and will, if informed, endeavour to make corrections in any future edition.
Top = t; Bottom = b; Centre = c; Left = l; Right = r
Cover © Chris van Rijswijk/Minden Pictures/FLPA; Page 3 ZSSD/Minden Pictures/FLPA; 4 Shutterstock/
Menno Schaefer; 5 Shutterstock/Gerrit de Vries; 6 Shutterstock/Peter Krejzl; 7 © Frans Lanting/Corbis;
8 Frans Lanting/FLPA; 9 Keving Elsby/FLPA; 10 Marcel can Kammen/Minden Pictures/FLPA;
11 © Wayne Lynch/All Canada Photos/Corbis; 12 Shutterstock/Bonnie Taylor Barry; 13t Shutterstock/
Butterfly Hunter; 13b David Hosking/FLPA; 14 Erica Olsen/FLPA; 15 Shutterstock/Andre Valado;
16 Shutterstock/Maslov Dmitry; 17 © DLLILLC Corbis; 18 Shutterstock/Delmas Lehman; 19 Shutterstock
/nice_pictures; 20 Shutterstock/Peter van Graafelland; 21t Shutterstock/Chris T Pehlivan; 21b Donald
M. Jones/Minden Pictures/FLPA; 22 Stefan Hewiler/Naturepl; 23 Dietmar Nill/Naturepl; 24 Dave Watts/
Naturepl; 25 Phil Savoie/Naturepl; 26–27 Getty images/Kerstin Waurick; 28 Getty images/Kerstin
Waurick; 29 Getty images /Kerstin Waurick; 30l Shutterstock/Doug Lemke; 30r Shutterstock/Daniel
Herbert; 31 Shutterstock/Doug Lemke

Birds are in the sky.

Birds are in the water.

Birds are on the ground.

Birds are in trees.

Birds are even
in the coldest place
on Earth.

Birds are everywhere!

The ostrich is the biggest bird.

It is taller than
the tallest person!

It is much
heavier too.

The bee hummingbird
is the smallest bird.

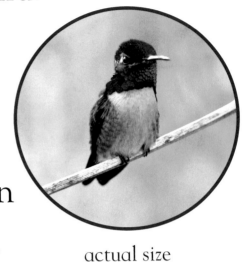

actual size

It is smaller than
most butterflies.

It weighs less than
two paper clips!

What makes an
animal a bird?

Feathers!

Birds are the
only animals
that have feathers.

Birds have different
kinds of feathers.

Most birds have strong,
stiff feathers on their wings
and tails.

These feathers help birds to fly.

Birds have soft
feathers.

These feathers
help a bird to
stay warm.

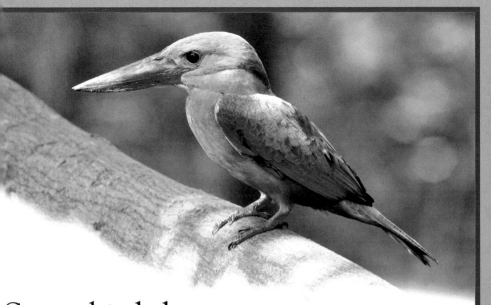

Some birds have
very bright feathers.

Some birds have feathers in
colours that help them to hide.

All birds have **wings**.

14

Most birds fly.
They use their wings to fly.

They spread their wings wide
and push up into the air.

Some birds that can fly
can swim too.

Webbed feet help them
to swim.

Some birds cannot fly.

Penguins are birds
that cannot fly.

Penguins use their wings
to swim!

Webbed feet help them
to swim too.

Some birds fly away
when winter comes
each year.

They fly back in the spring.

The Arctic tern
can fly further than
any other bird.

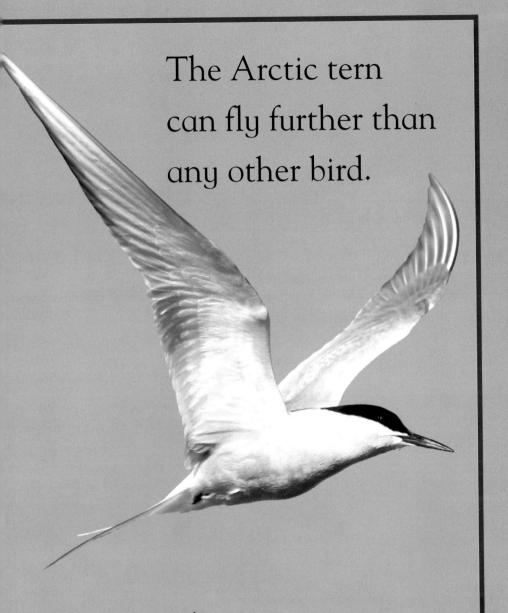

It flies more than
70,900 kilometres in a year!

All birds have a **beak**.

A bird's beak is the right size
and the right shape
for the kind of food it eats.

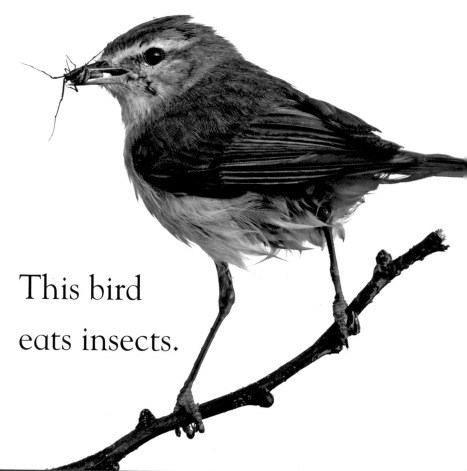

This bird
eats insects.

This bird
eats seeds.

This bird catches fish
with its beak.

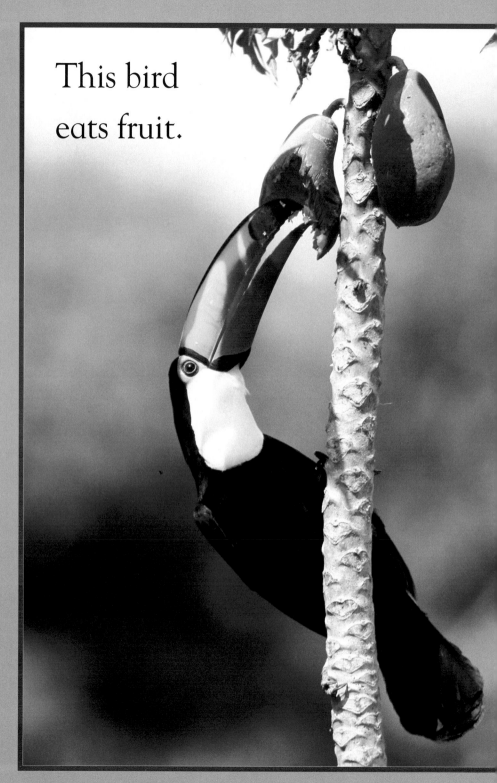

This bird
eats fruit.

This bird catches
and eats other animals.

When it is time to find a **mate**, most male birds try to get a female bird to notice them.

Some male birds dance to get noticed!

Some male birds
show their colours
to get noticed.

Every bird begins life inside an egg.

Most mother birds lay eggs in a **nest**.

After a few weeks,
the eggs **hatch**.

Most baby birds
are born without feathers.

They cannot see.

Their parents bring them food
and keep them warm.

When they are two weeks old, most baby birds have feathers and can see.

They are called **fledglings**.

When they are five weeks old, most birds are ready to learn how to fly.

They will soon be ready to leave the nest.

Birds are everywhere.

There may be birds
outside your window
right now.

Just take a look!

Glossary

beak the mouth of a bird

feathers thin coverings over a bird's body that keep it warm and dry. Feathers help a bird to fly, hide and find a mate.

fledglings young birds that are almost ready to fly

hatch to break out of an egg and be born

mate an animal partner; two mates have babies together

nest a home in which birds have their babies and look after them

webbed feet feet with a flap of skin between each toe

wings the parts of a bird's body that it uses to fly